GRA

GREEN

STOCKINGS

BY

MARION CARMICHAEL

ISBN 978-1-5272-2243-4

Published by
Rew Lane Books, Ventnor, Isle of Wight

Printed by Biltmore Printers, Newport, Isle of Wight

CONTENTS

CONTENTS

MIDSUMMER PICNIC

Oh yes, and bring a poem

A poem? I can't make a poem.
If only she'd asked for a pie...

Flirty flan with fluted edge
double crust with crisp gold top
pale, creamy quiche
cross hatched with succulent
asparagus.
Filo tartlets soft and crunchy
oozing warm mozzarella over sun-dried tomatoes
olives, basil, roasted pine-nuts;
or dripping sweetness from
ripe firm-fleshed, purple plums
sexy apricots with their
rosy round bums;
blood red raspberries
mouthing perfumed promises.
Rich choux buns in dark pools
of melting chocolate.

Any of these I would make for her
but a poem?
If only she'd asked for a pie.

TIME TO LEAVE TOWN

But why Biggleswade? They laugh
sipping trendy cocktails through a straw.

Do I tell them?
Of flat fields of sprouts
fog heavy days
slow speech, dull houses,
brickworks and Bunyan.

Reaching for the olives, he says:
No one goes to Biggleswade.

And he's right
the Great North Road
now a motorway
bypasses the town
known only for tractors and bikes.

Shaking her shining straight hair
she asks: *Where is it? In the Fens?*

No. There are no
whispering reeds
no watery reflections
glimpsed in changeful light.
Nothing so mysterious.

What will you do in the evenings?
sneers my erstwhile lover.

I remember nights
of iron hard frost
winter skies crowded with stars.
And how winds, let loose from Siberia,
howl, grief stricken
at street corners.

You will be back.

Oh yes, I give you...
six months max.

Same again, everyone?

Ah Biggleswade!

WHAT I DID THIS SUMMER

What to say of summer twenty thirteen?
When I did nothing and nothing happened.
The kindest thing would be an empty page
not attempt to create a story from:
events I did not enjoy, sun drenched days
not spend on the beach, glorious sunsets
I never saw, mainland friends who didn't visit
the loving family who had better things to do
and stayed away. Festival tickets
I couldn't afford, Invites to garden
parties and barbecues that never arrived.

My passport languishes in the drawer
cheap souvenirs I never bought don't
make me smile as they gather dust or remind
me of seafood I never tasted, served
on rickety tables, that didn't rock for me,
gingham oilcloth stained by cheap red wine
I didn't drink, on the terrace where
I didn't watch the velvet night brighten
with diamond stars. No dark voiced young men
eager to serve my food, fill my glass, spin
me any tale I wanted to hear.

No. I stayed here on the Island, broke a bone
could not drive, spent hours on Vectis buses
and many more waiting for them to arrive.
Witnessed the casual cruelty of narrow minded
locals and bone headed visitors, saw prices
rise and rain fall, overheard a woman say
she loved all the little silly seaside shops.
Most played safe, clogged Newport streets in their quest
for Marks, Next or Tesco's familiar doors.
I searched in vain for 'Island' strawberries
took home raspberries grown in Aberdeen.

GRASS GREEN STOCKINGS

Had I known of Joyce Jeffreys on the long gone
day of the green, knee high socks
my whole life could have been different.

No longer wrong footed outsider
as her acolyte I would have asserted
my right to live as she did:
alone, managing her money, reading
where she wished. No man's footnote.

She gave her godchild a coat made
from scarlet wool, to each of her maids a
shilling to spend at the Lady Day Fair

letting *them* choose to buy pretty ribbons
watch a horse dance, give a penny
to the man with the monkey?
Joyce Jeffreys bought an ounce of
good *tobacko*, smoked her pipe.

Always wore grass green stockings.

Business and Household Accounts of
Joyce Jeffreys, Spinster of Hereford, 1638 -1648.
edited by Judith Spicksley
March 2013

11th OCTOBER SHEFFORD FAIR DAY

Traffic banned streets overflow with
make-shift stalls, roundabouts, smells
of fried onions and candy floss.

Generators churn raw energy
and noise: *Beatles, Madonna, Blur.*
Coloured light-bulbs boogie in the wind.

Rides scream and whirl, dodgems crash
goldfish gape, wait for hoop-la rings
coconuts wobble as balls thwack.

Out of reach, pink teddies beckon.
Dark, burnt-sugar smell of sweet stalls
spit-rock, humbugs, toffee-apples.

Roll-up, Roll-up three shots a pound!

Hinged wooden ducks 'swim' round and round
young men swagger, take aim - **Crack, Crack
Crack,** ducks sail on Quack, Quack, Quack.

Swing boats creak. Velvet covered ropes stretch....
fall. Her eyes shine, he grins they fly above
the town they fly into the starlit sky.

LEVEL CROSSING

Spitting fire
train roars
between trembling gates
rails scream
footbridge shakes
every bolt and hinge rattles.

The bus shudders.
From the top deck eyes strain
through breath smeared windows.

The crossing keeper's shadow
dangles by the swinging light
of a single electric bulb
huge black marionette jerks
spins the great wheel
red circles split, the gates open.

We jolt over the tracks
travel on to meat pie and cabbage
in Bedford, Hitchin or Biggleswade.

The train flames on across dark fields
to York, Durham, Edinburgh.

BACK THEN

After Gill Learner

Tell me about winter nights, drawn curtains, closed doors,
ghost stories, crackling sticks, bread on the long
toasting fork, hot butter dribbling down your chin.
Describe the smell of apple wood, explain blue flames
trapped in shiny coal, how green logs spit, drying clothes steam.

Tell me how bees make candles, explain snuff, wick, trim,
the quiet oval glow; how flickering flames made shapes
black and scary when you climbed the draughty stairs
shapes that danced around your bed, would not let you sleep.
Explain strike a match, how the tiny head explodes in a whoosh of light.

Tell me about a kettle that sings on the hearth
describe how to control the heat of a range
hot for scones and pastry, cool for custard or fish
and keep it steady for Sunday dinner, Wednesday's stew.
Explain chopping wood, the daily clearing of ash.

Tell me about a heap of rubbish raked high
describe roar like the wind, smoke curls, tatters in the sky.
Explain dry stalks, wet grass, prunings, turning leaves.
Tell about that autumn smell and in the embers
jacket potatoes, burning skin creamy white flesh.

Tell me about when heat and light came raw, dangerous,
lively. Describe fire before all power was switched.

CIVIC CELEBRATIONS

Dull, well drilled they stand in line
a measured distance from the road.
Council soldiers pebble dashed
stout defenders of back gardens
overflowing with runner beans
roses, washing lines, bicycles
sweet peas, currant bushes, marrows
cabbages, children and chickens.
Fronted by regulation squares
of forlorn grass and gateless hedge
poor relations, kept clean and decent
to fend off gossip and shame.

Then pictures of the new Queen
on stamps, mugs, coins and toffee tin
lids. Street parties, flags everywhere.
the Council caught the spirit of the age,
seduced by marshmallow pink blossoms,
a lorry load of saplings arrives
one for the front of each house.
Right in the middle of each uniform
square the strangers dig deep holes
plant, stake, tie, label every tree.
Chuck their tools into the lorry
rattlebang out of the village.

Every year since, at winter's
parting blast fine pink lace is torn
on thorns, bedraggled, footprinted
with mud, each stylish designer
clad flower destroyed, overtaken
by drab scullery maid leaves
the exotic vision become
appropriate rent payers' trees
drowning both garden and house
in a mournful gloom of deep shade.

Fifty wind battered springs go by.
The cherry trees grow tall and wide
until the whole village decide
on a new scheme, a golden plan
several men arrive in a van.
At the end of the day the trees
are gone, crazy paving buries
the ground they used to darken
bright shiny cars and some old heaps
safe, off the road parked before
their owners pebble dashed homes.

SHORTEST DAY TAKEAWAY

Five days to Christmas
strings of fairy lights
like mosquito bites
sting the damp morning
windscreen wipers
slice grey drizzle.

Huddles of stunted trees
straggle the coast road
crocodile clouds sink
in car park puddles
mist stained cliffs drip
like dirty linen.

Brakes bite, car stops
the engine dies.
Low beams of sunlight
fray the clouds
parcel the waves
with silver ribbons.

Spinach and ricotta oozes
from flaky pastry, dribbles
onto the paper bag
green lettering weeps
sticks to the polystyrene cup
of cooling black tea.

On the beach below
two dogs run free dash
splash, into the waves.
Coloured like next week's
turkey stock, the sea
swirls round, stirs over.

CHANCE STOP ON A JOURNEY

There were changes. Fifty years
of course there were changes:
school yard brimming with houses
post office reduced to *The Old Post Office*
inscribed on a wrought iron plaque.
The Corner Shop, Miss Goddard's
The Fish Shop all gone.

> Streets keep to their ancient ways
> lead to the village well, long since become
> the War Memorial, pale, fading lists
> of Clifton men lost to world wars
> joined now by dark new carving
> names not known to me, lives cut short
> in Bosnia, Iraq, Afghanistan.

Clipped yews guard the Lychgate,
same crunch of gravel takes me
to Church where the gentle shepherd
still waits with his crook above the porch door,
backdrop to countless photographs.
Beside the wall headstones lean
grass grows thick over chapter and verse.

> Deep shade fills the lane down to the river
> where once lines of willow trees, stood
> grown for cricket bats. A riot of grasses
> and cow parsley bend in the wind.
> The unremarkable river; scene of
> picnics, pooh sticks, settling of old scores,
> well known 'secret' meeting place for lovers

reflects the wide arc of the sky; winds through
flat fields green and golden with summer crops.
Small birds dart about, insects and bees buzz
a bike freewheels down the hill, the rider
a white haired woman, helmetless
in sensible skirt and short sleeved shirt,
waves to me as she pedals on.

> Leaning on the river bridge
> broken stones warm my hand, I look and *see*
> *understand* this dull land's quiet colours
> it's wide spaces stretching from Shefford
> across to Stanford, feel the bite of ice
> in today's summer wind, watch, wise women
> wave riding their bikes, shout *Good Morning.*

Deep in my bones, more than memory,
a thread tugs tight in my life's tapestry.

POSTCARD FROM THE SEASIDE

Three jolly nuns in deck chairs are sitting
While one reads a book another is knitting
The last of the three watches where sky and sea mingle
Slowly curls her toes in the deep cool shingle.

And so they sit, these virgins wise
Protected by a brake from the blasts and prying eyes.
The one who was knitting is now eating chips
The next, paperback finished, her ninety nine licks.

But the one in the middle smiles gently and dreams
As her stiff knees relax in the sun's warm beams.
She hears, far away, the sea's clatter and sigh
Tastes salt on her tongue as the day slips by.

THE RUNNING THREAD

In isolated villages, tumble-
down cottages lean, sink into the earth.
Women cut short strips from: patched breeches;
torn skirts; old petticoats worn to rags.
For backing: wash, trim, shape a cast aside sack.
Sort the strips and with a wooden peg thread
them through the sackcloth, knot each one tight,
keep the strips close pile them thick as thieves.
When the snow blows in the door Ma's rag rug
warms frozen feet clustered near the low fire.

Towns built of red brick terraced houses
long straight streets stretching over the hills.
Women wind skeins of wool, treasure crochet hooks,
long wooden needles that click clack, click clack,
by candle lit fireside, on front door steps
under pale summer stars they knit. Mufflers
kind as Christmas, wind defying jerseys,
itchy vests and socks. For newborns
they crochet blankets, bootees and bonnets
for grandmamas enveloping shawls, rugs
to tuck around stiff, rheumaticky knees.

Suburban semi's, lawn set and fenced
wait for *Janet and John* to return.
Women buy *Vogue* paper patterns, cut pieces
from cotton cloth, pin, tack. Threading needles
winding bobbins their *Singer* treadles fly:
french seams, set in sleeves, smocking, ruffles, frills,
pleats, zipps, hooks and eyes, button holes hand stitched.
Summer dresses, winter coats, shirts and skirts.
They make and line curtains, bedspreads and blinds.
Their homes, children and themselves all sewn up.

Glass and steel apartments soar, where every
balcony, watches the river wind to the sea
women tweet, tap into the internet,
log on to Facebook trawl through ebay sites
restless they search ease dissatisfactions,
pent up fury at global trade, ready
made, here today gone tomorrow, *Must Have
Fashion*. In despair Google retro-sites.
haunt charity shops search for patterns
needles, wool and crochet hooks.

RAIN-WASHED, AUTUMN MORNING

Rain-washed autumn morning
glorious day.

A condom on the road
slack and spent.

Suburban feet give it a
wide berth...

but hear its raucous shout
of lust and life.

Violent, loud, careless
or carefree?

A threat

that penetrates
tidy neat-garden lives

behind double locked
front doors.

Forces open the fault lines
of hidden dreams.

MERENGUE

I thought you said merengue
came in flirty skirt and heels
you wanted a pavlova.
Lunch party ruined
our friendship over.

PLAIN SPEAKING

Our northern friend
calls an arse and arse
regardless of who owns it:
no bum for mates
bottom for babies
behind for those with nothing
between waist and thighs
no derriere for aunts
or posterior for someone he really dislikes.

This in not for me, give me a man
unafraid of euphemisms.
Who calls me his gorgeous darling
when I behave like a fishwife
look like an unmade bed.

PASSING BY

having seen Bridget
her brown tee shirt
and curly hair
I knew it would be alright
I watched the sun
twinkle on her glasses
could not decide
which reflected what
her dancing eyes
or the bright April sun

how right to meet
her in the afternoon
a time for gentle exchanges
tea, scones, casual sex...

IT IS ONLY A SPOON!

She held it close.

Knew he was right. But, the spoon
had shown her the difference
between level, rounded, heaped

How and when to fold, stir or beat.
Measured porridge, treacle, rice
plain flour for sauces, sugar for

Custard. Served shepherd's pie,
curry, carrots. The spoon always
reliable, never moody

Or unaccountably late home.
Forgotten before the meal is
eaten, left in the kitchen when

The music starts, the fun begins.
Only a spoon? Only a woman,
she pulls on her coat, pockets the spoon.

AFTER SUPPER

Rings tell their stories
hand-wrought by a lover
one protects, keeps secrets.
Precious woven metals
yellow, white and rose
make a cradle for tears.
Everyday wedding bands
shine through their scratches.
on the third finger of one hand
a faint blue shadow.

GIRL SUSPENDED

Her fingers claw
the music room roof
terrified teachers pray
she will not fall

on the ridge she dances
two fingers school
and teachers
dares them to come to her

police arrive
take her away
teachers rearrange their faces
the Head completes the form.

....

Years later I see her.
Fierce hurt angry
each long stride a cry.
I ask how things are?

Good, she says
next year will be good
new place, new course,
fresh start.

I nod and smile
wish her luck.
Her face softens
pretty in the sun

she's read the book
I lent her
says, *it's cool*
we talk of others.

Tall, fearless, thin
she strides on.
Baby clouds blow about
the back-street sky.

On a row of Cloakroom Pegs
hang white school shirts
reception class to 'A' level.
Inside each collar, neatly stitched
Cash's Woven Name Tapes
tell a story. No names
but memories
words whispered,
shouted, casually spoken
at children who wore
shirts such as these.
Children In Care.

STOP being so lazy!
STOP annoying me!
STOP doing your bloody make-up!

For God's sake stop crying.
As usual you're lying.
Don't bother trying.

You're not going to be anything.
You're not a little girl any more.
If you can't afford a pen?

Don't bother trying.
For God's sake stop crying.
As usual you're lying.

Calm down you.
It's all your fault.
Don't come in here.

As usual YOU'RE lying
DON'T bother trying.
For God's sake STOP crying.

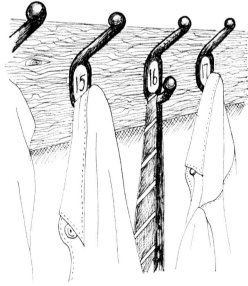

WONG TAI SIN

Every wish comes true upon request
in the *Make a Wish Garden*
at Wong Tai Sin

we walk
find a bench, watch
the waters of the lake

on the jade roof tiles
of the temple
a golden dragon sleeps

worshippers kneel
shake bundles
of sticks

sweet smoke
uncurls, incense and prayers
pattern the sky.

Carefully we choose, buy
three perfect oranges
place them on the altar

an offering,
a gift, for
Past Present and Future

In little booths hung about
with good omens
fortune tellers wait

we hesitate... sit
surrender our hands
to be read.

He says,
The future is good
we ask, How long?

he shrugs, folds
pencilled notes into
green and red envelopes.

Later I hold her hand until
she sleeps; the fortune teller's
envelope under her pillow

Alone on the balcony
I weep; hear the gibbons
howling at the coming dark.

NO EPITHALAMIUM

No Bridal Song for you
who, no blushing bride
leapt from partner
to married woman in ten minutes.

Your lunch hour wedding
in a back room
witnessed by two strangers
it's legal. Now, return to work.

One to meet and greet, One to the office.

No flowers or guests,
no music, no rings exchanged.
You told no one. The so important certificate
carefully filed away.

There were moments
when you were teased
passing years, *will you ever make it legal,
isn't it time?*

Did you catch his eye and smile?

You told us on that dreadful last day
and despite all, we laughed
we three standing round
you on a hospital trolley.

As if in sudden sunlight
we laughed with joy,
between hugs and kisses
we chide you like naughty children.

A baffled nurse casts an anxious eye.

Today, this ancient church is full
of flowers, familiar music
so many friends gather,
together we sing your Requiem.

UNKNOWN WOMAN

She waters the plants He loved to grow
red and yellow peppers, aubergines,
small hot chillies she once made into
tabbouleh, humus, meals they shared.
Their daughter skips, rope thwacks down on hot stone.
He loves you, he loves you not, he loves you.
The boy drives his toy cars in circles; grins to
Mother and Sister; has never seen his Father.

A chair waits for HIM shaded by the tree.
She knows the strong man they took from her
will not return. She remembers his smile
seen every day in the eyes of their son;
pictures his body, straight, hard, beautiful.
Dares not think of what they may have done
have yet to do to him, alone in the
filthy dark, hidden from the world's sight.

AUGUST

Holiday traffic clogs motorways and narrow lanes
hot queues form in airports and terminals
like a reluctant guest, summer slips away,

Busy spiders barricade garden gates
deceitful light hides swell of ripening apples.
Conkers, blackberries peer from heat heavy leaves.

As our harvest comes home the year closes
on families torn apart, lives destroyed
by wars unstoppable, insane. It's then

winter comes to the desert, and there
in the star-filled night, for want of a
blanket new-born, summer-born babies die.

BRITAIN APRIL 2015

Today
in the middle of town
on a park bench
today
a man died

nothing suspicious
natural causes
cold, hunger,
loneliness, despair.
A Man Died

today
in the park
in the middle of town
on a bench
a man died.

NEXT OF KIN

The door opens
welcomes us
to their tragedy
we talk of the boys
look at photos
listen, shocked and useless.

She says, *He is safe*
nothing can hurt him now.
When I see him
he will still be young and strong.
Just like he was.

We look away.

He says, *No*
I don't think like that.
When a rose shatters
it is lost
forever.

ALVERSTONE MEAD

Alverstone   Alverstone   Lowland
Alverstone   Alverstone   Meadland
Alverstone Mead Alverstone Mead Grassland
                                Wetland

Alverstone Mead.

Water flows
Water winds
Water snakes down to the sea

Look along the riverbank

Perch roach and sticklebacks
swim in the river
dazzling demoiselle dragonflies
use the fringing reeds
climb out of the water
to dance in the sun.

Willow warblers and fly catchers feast
on the buzz around the overhanging trees.
A solitary kingfisher dives
scatters diamonds on the sunlit water.
Yellow flag iris and purple comfrey
splash colour across the deep green banks
meadowsweet and water mint scent
the soft summer air.

Wetland
Lowland
Grassland
Meadland

Alverstone Mead

Rain falls
Puddles form
Water cups in the leaves of trees

Look over to the woods.

On the higher, drier ground
runs Borthwood Lynch
oak, hazel and cherry trees
form this ancient boundary ridge
among the climbing corydalis and ragged robin
badgers travel their timeworn paths.

The damp margins of the mead are thick with
ferns, sedges, bright marsh marigolds
shade dapples through the broad leaves
wood crickets scrape a thin song
great spotted woodpeckers
hammer away at tree trunks where
serotine bats roost and little owls make
their burrows. Acorns, hazel nuts, woodland
berries nourish the sleepy dormouse.

Meadland
Wetland
Lowland
Grassland

Alverstone Mead

Water floods
Water drains
Water stands in marshy pools

Look across to the wet meadow.

The narrow crisscrossing ditches
loved by water rail, wood cock
and timid water voles
wetland plants marshwort, woundwort,
bird's foot trefoil and pennywort
support all the life of the mead.

In winter elephant trunk drains
flood the mead protect the grassland.
When the trunk is lowered ditchwater
runs into the river, the meadow dries
lush grasses grow tall and sweet
dotted with pink ladies smocks
jigsaw patterned cows stand udder
deep, sleep in the chewy heat.

Barn owls and little owls hunt
by a handful of pale summer stars.

Grassland
Wetland
Meadland
Lowland

Alverstone Mead

Alverstone
Alverstone
Alverstone Mead.

NEWTOWN

High water slaps on rough stone walls
washing lines dinghy hung creak, stretch
across mirrored clouds sea cradled
an egret flaps from the old salt pans
a curlew calls across the long sea marsh.

In the meadow timothy grass bows
tall fescues dressed with ladies-smocks
and daisies hold a garden party
for pale blue butterflies and loud bees
a blackbird sings from trees at the field's edge.

Once Vikings slashed through brambles and briars
now dog roses shatter on Jill Pike's bench.

MARGARET ON A BENCH

Julia Margaret played with light
turned urchins into angels, conjured
stories from shadows. Here sunlight slides
round the shade of short days, night dark shadows
paddle your blue feet; winter sun dazzles,
shuts your eyes. Sepia grasses squeeze
memories of summer; fickle as frogs
they leap, dance in the wind, shift in the light.
Impatient, in your warm earth-coloured coat,
your hand ready to slice walnut cake, pour
strong flasked tea to steam in the cold air.
Beside you the photographer's bag gapes
waits, like a cradle while the camera
taking your picture plays tricks with the light.

BENCHES

Give thanks for the sturdy hard working bench.
Out in all weathers: legs gnawed by rabbits
defaced by louts and lovers, ensnared
by trailing weeds, scent marked by foxes, a
scratching post for badgers and hapless drunks
gouged by falling bikes, scraped by muddy boots,
stand-in picnic table stained, sticky with
salad cream, ketchup, and spilt lemonade.
A simple shape they're welcomed by tired
walkers who sit - rest, enjoy the view
stretch then start anew. Like a loyal hound
undemanding, always around, blest
with the knack of being where they're needed
as if they grow like dock-leaves by nettles.

COUNTRY COTTAGE

Aunt Jinny would skin and clean
snared rabbits, to make a pie or a stew.
And I couldn't ride home on my bike
after drinking her sweet damson wine.

This pretty chocolate box cottage,
made me think of her house.
It too was thatched, built long and low
and sideways to the road.

Sheltered by a busy hawthorn hedge
smudgy white broad bean flowers
rubbed shoulders with crimson peonies.
Beetroot grew beside sweet scented pinks.

Under its heavy brows of thatch
the house sat, sulky and squat
hunched against the winter storms,
hiding from the summer heat.

The rising sun came in at the back door
bitter winds blew in from the Steppes.
A black range scowled at the floor
while the dinner struggled to cook.

Evening light rested in the parlour
crammed with stiff horsehair sofa
hard wooden chairs, a round table,
some laughter a few ornaments and tears.

Pleasing, useful, reminiscent
of beam engines and milk churns.
Two watering cans hang on a red brick wall.

Elsewhere they make holes in
long grass growing free in
weedy corners where

taps perch on metal pipes
ready to rattle gush a rainbow
into these heavy old cans.

Ghosts drift in the misty day
slight women in crochet gloves
and shady hats lift the cans

the hems of their skirts
damp from wet grass
and spilt water.

They bend, tend the graves of lost loves
plant snowdrops, arrange sweet peas.
Shadows fall, reflections shift

I see aunts, sisters, my Mother, myself
low winter sun lights the headstones.
A lost butterfly spreads her wings.

THE SMELL OF CIGARETTES AND STRAW

After supper, at Harvest Time, you leave
go back to the fields, work on, come home late
ride your bike through the heavy summer dark.

Lying in bed sweet smelling sheets scrape my
sunburnt shoulders. From the street I hear the
shouts of other children. Allowed to stay out

they are playing hopscotch. A small thud when
the stone falls, then the flat smack of sandals
shrieks as someone wobbles on one leg.

I twist about, too hot to sleep. sit up
reach under the bed, slide onto the floor
find it, jump back read Anne of Green Gables...

Dusty, tired you come, whisper Good Night
smile, wink as you move the half-hidden book
your stubble scratches my cheek, I breath
the smell of cigarettes and straw.

Bent low
face hidden in the shade
of your hat

your arm stretches forward
shirt sleeve rolled
up tense muscle, tanned skin

elbow swings back
marble white your upper arm
shocks.

you grip worn wood
the moon blade
splinters green spikes into rough stalks.

In the barn the sickle hangs
high on the whitewashed wall
you rake grass into low heaps

I spread a blanket
taste sweet scented sweat
on your hot skin.

LADY IN A FLOWER SHOP

You are *Eliza's, Lady in a Flower Shop*
elegant as a Madonna lily
pale as winter primroses
you stand all day in a cold shop
your wet hands torn by
thorns and woody stems.

You turn unruly blossoms
into love tokens,
apologies, thanks.
your blue fingers conjure
eloquent messengers
from dumb vegetation.

The sad find comfort in your flowers
hiding behind your red roses
shy suitors take heart
new fathers say everything
through your delicate sprays
each bride is promised joy.

But you weave a warning
into gaudy overpriced
philandering bouquets.

LONDON 'LATIONS

The circus has come to town.
Glass cracking voices, rib crushing hugs
sparkly earrings, flash dresses, scarlet lipstick
the house shrinks as they gobble up the air.

They know everything.
Gadgets, easy food, stylish clothes
all are paraded for us to see.
Jokes spin above my head like plates,
fat aunts wobble
dodgy uncles slap their thighs and wink
stick thin cousins screech
babies, passed like popcorn, gurgle.

Mum smiles all the time
everyone talks...
even Dad joins in

until

under a spotlight moon
their hooting car
carries them

away

CITY LIFE - LONDON 1914

After Gill Learner

Tell me about walking London's dawn-dark streets to
Covent Garden's Floral Hall, the riot of paint-box
colours; air heavy with perfume lilies, roses.
Describe heaving boxes of flowers up the stairs
of an open top, horse drawn omnibus.

Sing the songs from *Chu Chin Chow,* tell how you queued
in the rain for seats in the *Gods.* Describe watching
the *Air Show* where biplanes looped the loop, the muddy
field, your friend teetering in her *hobble skirt.*

Tell me about strangers, how talking schoolgirl French
you met home-sick soldiers. Say more about Southend
how all night the sound of the guns echoed across
the sea and how daylight took you back to London.

Describe when you all ran from your houses to see
Zeppelins low over the city, scared their bombs
would fall on your street. Tell again how planes shoot, gas
explodes and men *all alight* fall through the night sky.

WRITING A BIOGRAPHY

You queue with me
to post Christmas parcels
tut about spoilt children.

Shop with me
in supermarket aisles
sniff at suspicious
foreign vegetables.

Smile
as I drive us home.

You walk with me
through a harvest field
watch the sun unwrap
hedge hidden dog roses.

I catch your glance
in my son's questioning look.

Hear you weep
in the pitiless dawn
cradling the ache
for your lost daughters.

Recognize you in my
granddaughter's trusting hand.

Laugh with you
by the crackle of a February fire
when you try to hide your pride
in your two strong sons.

Fear your legendary anger
if I get this wrong.

Do So Want
your nod of approval
if I get it *half right*.

NEW BRIDGE AT NEWTOWN

Lop-sided, lame the old bridge at Newtown
limped from salt marsh to hay-meadow
railway sleeper and chicken wire causeway
licked and lapped by each high tide
natural as egret's flight, curlew's cry.

Now orange varnish glitters from chunky
wooden posts, scars the marsh, blights the skyline.
I hear a cuckoo call from the copse
late primroses watch the sun, a small field
shelters a flock of black sheep and their lambs.

You call from Australia make me laugh
remind me why bridges are repaired
kept strong to carry home flocks of black sheep
stretch long to reach every wayward cuckoo.

THE VISIT

The plane turns, banks, races down...to kisses
the same grin your laughing eyes that rhyme.
Now I know you're glad I came, our hands touch
as we walk to your home. A single noun
says this is your front door. I am to have the bed
you will sleep on the floor. We eat outside
drink beer, you tell me of your new romance
the plump olives sharp on my tongue, we talk
as the warm darkness covers the square,
relax easy in our old love.
I watch: your hands, the way you turn your head
think of these things as I lie in your bed.

FIGURE OF SPEECH

Angela Carter wrote: *Mother*
is just a figure of speech.
I thought of this as I walked
down the aisle
of Mothers' Day cards.
Cards I have not bought
for twenty one years.

I remembered old Charlie Albone.
Who every spring turned
his front garden into
a golden sea of daffodils
that he sold for 9d a dozen.

People went that way
on their Sunday walks
to *OOH! and AHH!*
Compare the crop with others
maybe buy a bunch.
Each stem snapped with a clear crack
the sweet sap oozing
like blood.

When I was seventeen
my first year at work
I asked Mr Albone
to pick you a fanfare
of twelve trumpeting bunches.

On Mothering Sunday morning
he piled the flowers
in my bicycle basket
and I rode them home to you
I see your dancing eyes
as I came round the corner
you said: *You are a naughty girl*
to spend all your money.

We both knew that was
just a figure of speech.

ROSES

A basket of roses on the front porch?
Small milkmaid faces smile
from thick green hair.

Days later wilting leaves tell me
that they too are weary.
Post operative tears fall
when I see their strangled roots
twisted like cold spaghetti.

A pot of cool earth,
gentle watering, light feeding
and the beneficent sun
make fingernail buds thicken.
New leaves uncurl.

Planted out
five glossy bushes
strong and straight
they take their place
among the hebes and lavender.

All summer they bloom
soft pink and deep clotted cream
their fat, flat faces follow the sun
until sweet nicotianas open
swallows swoop across the violet sky.

On this new year morning
late pink and cream revellers
straggle across dark leaves.

PICNIC

Now we are six, picnics are a problem.
Your brothers keep asking

When? Please When?
When can we have a picnic?

They say, *It's not the same in the garden.*
We want to go away, for the whole day.

Oh Pleeease When?
When can we have a picnic?

We went to the park, for all of the day.

Bags and bottles
cricket stumps and a football
pork pies and lemonade
flapjack and jelly
all piled into your smart
coach built pram.

You were wedged in with rugs and sun hats
sitting on your rainbow blanket
under the ragged fringe of
the green lined canopy
in your bag pureed carrots
and a banana.

The sun shone.

We played rounders
the boys rolled
down the hill
played cricket
raced about
rowed on the lake.

Stretched on the grass
we ate as we pleased
beside us you slept
spread like a star on your blanket.

MUD CLINGS TO THE WHEELS
OF HIS BIKE

As he careers
round and round
the yard

puddles splash
leave earth coloured
streaks
on his bare legs

they whirl like
egg beaters
faster and faster.

He hits a hidden brick

CRASHES.

I kiss
his bloody knee
his round tear spattered
cheeks

we rescue the
upended
undamaged bike.

He smiles
green eyes
bright

rides a careful circle
steers
avoids the puddles
takes control.

Passes through
the gate, rides out, far
beyond the yard.

LOST BOYS

I cannot tell how much I love you.
How precious still you are.
How strange it seems now you are gone
now my orbit has lost its star.
I did not know how the house would mourn
as the silence settles deep.
Did not know for just how long
our cat, would his lonely vigil keep.
Did not know what sorrow is in the sea's soft sigh
how the chalk Downs turn away
at the seagulls echoing cry
the migrant shape of geese
against the darkening sky.

ROCKING CHAIR

Easter Sunday
your Christening Day
a great party
who took the photograph
of you and your Grandmother?

White paint gleams.
Unseen, tea-stained rockers
scarred legs
unpainted seat
hidden by a cushion.

Today I write to you
scratched arms cradle me
rockers, legs and seat
still unpainted...

TABLE SPOON

Scratched and wearing a bit thin
no longer fit for the table
the spoon gets lost in the back of the drawer.

Once I used it all the time,
every day measured porridge, pasta,
flour for a sauce, sugar for custard

From baby days to manhood,
cooking for our boys as my Mum
did when she cooked for me.

My brother and sisters, all
grew up, nourished by the spoon
beating batter puddings for Sunday

Dinner, then serving home grown
carrots, peas, tiny new potatoes
fresh dug that morning by our Dad.

The spoon taught me to measure the
difference between level, rounded and
heaped how and when to fold, stir, beat.

Will it be thrown out, sent
to a charity shop? Will someone
remember, hear stories it has to tell?

The granddaughter who likes history
and loves to cook, or the son who
often asks, *Where is Gran's spoon?*

WOMEN READING

When women read they disappear
don't hear, ignore demands for more
dissolve, grow wings of gossamer.

Leave unwashed socks on dirty floors
ride black stallions, drink cold gin
weep with Owen for the pity of war.

Shiver as snow falls on the living
and the dead. Stand firm with Germaine
o.d. on i.d. climb the thin

track to Xanadu. Don't explain
why they look like an unmade bed
or the spreading dark wine-red stain.

Manacles shatter as women read, slide
aside minds billowing like a rising tide.

WEEDING A POEM

Tendrils of thought
wind around my page
search for an idea
grow from the dense
prose of the borders

I pull up punctuation
root out adjectives
dead-head seedy adverbs

Iambics rhyme in late afternoon sun
rhythmic fountains plash in ferny pools
Italian marble steps lead up and round
where tender couplets grow in fertile ground

LIFE ON THE PATIO

We write in the cracks of our lives
tiny fault lines between mother and wife
where strong verbs take root
polysyllabic phrases wither in the dark
crevices narrow, fill with wasted time and chores
others disappear the border lost
between sister and friend
some: daughter, teacher gape wide
reveal seedling poems, rambling stories
great clumps of novels.

couplet
quatrain
assonance
sonnet
Ode
alliteration
haiku
Stanza
rhyme
FLOUR
A.C. McG 2018

HER HEAD IS RANSACKED

Drawers are overturned

Files emptied
heaps of paper
litter the floor

Laughing children, faces ripped
squint from shattered frames

Mother's pearls roll unstrung
under upended chairs

Splintered legs rock

Shadow-puppet fingers
point at dark graffiti
sprayed over calendar notes
and gossiping postcards

Father's silver cup
battered, misshapen
his name, Best In Show
obscured by grime

Broken backed books
private parts displayed
moan quietly
as each
torn page
floats
to the floor.

M.E. is me

Zigzag cracks
ice breaking
on an inland sea

Light refracted
from jagged glass

Dazzles splinters
in rainbow jokes, sharp
as the sting of nettles

Each diamond moment
framed by a chasm
that drags

Bends elbows,
ankles, knees
to crazy-mirror distortions

Sinews scream
stretched
down

Down
to where
transparent creatures
blind plastic bags
drift
aimless as dust

The broken mess
shudders

Kaleidoscopic jangle
of suffocating rooms
breath wrenching blizzards

That swallow
and spit

Random
as the wind

That

Steals a child's balloon...

CHRONIC FATIGUE

Alone in my monochrome world
helpless months and years drag by
lethargy wraps around my head
I'm the mummy that cannot die.
The world goes on, I feel it fly
left behind I wait and grieve
unable either to speak or cry.

Just enough energy to breath.

The sun breaks through like a prism
shatters the dark, dazzles my eye
the gate clangs back on my prison
in my mind the tiny seeds lie.
Hope glimmers, flickers to a sigh
Cheap trickery the light deceives
as all the colours drain and die.

Just enough energy to breath.

ALL WINTER THE COAT LANGUISHED

Behind the back door
three buttons lost
the last one hanging by a thread
she shivered in her old mac
wore the grubby fleece
with a broken zip

One empty afternoon
she found a card of buttons
thin February sun licked
their mottled plastic

She stitched as the light
leached from her window
the needle stabbing
dragging pale cotton
through stained fabric
round and round

She wound a noose
tugged each shank
fastened off
snapped the final thread

BECOMING WALLPAPER

They gather in the cafe
wait
for her to stitch
a sequinned story
slice through the shit
with diamond edged
double sided wit
turn the question
that keys their padlocked pain

Today

She watches
their red fish mouths
as she flattens fades snaps the chain

On the wallpaper a spreading stain

WOLVES PROTECT THE MEDITATION GROUP

A shifting circle of lean shadows
separates the mad and the therapist
tails down, teeth bared, sharp eyes watchful
low warning growls fortress the space
keep safe the besieged
as dead theories fly
from academic trebuchet
articulate arrows scorch the air
ladders of logic, twibils of talk
beat down on the lonely lunatics
muscles bunch, the wolves leap...

PENCILS

Obedient
I take one
from the box
smell its woody newness
stroke smooth squared sides
recognise dark red paint
point leaden sharpness into my finger

Remember when I
ordered pencils like these
gave them to my class
each new-year
September morning

A voice says

Try to write your name
just your first name.

A nurse grips my hand
pencils clatter
falL..

Outside the frost lingers

THE VALUE OF GROUP WORK

Striped TIGERS hunt alone
Have no need for others.

Single LEOPARDS keep their spots
merge among the shadows.

Solitary POLAR BEARS vanish
on the white snow fields.

Timid DEER and SHEEP
herd and flock together.

THE SLOTH AND THE AGOUTI

Hey great day, Goot, said Sloth to Agouti.

I don't have time, Agouti replied.

Let it hang, man, loosen up, re-e-lax.

Too much to do, and if people like you...

Sloth rolled a smile, stopped to scratch awhile.

Agouti dashed up and down in a rage
worried about the end of the world.

Sloth unhooked one leg, kept the others curled.

Agouti counted to ten, then, his nerves in shreds
ran round in circles so they should not starve.

Sloth opened his eyes, *Cool it Goot, he sighed,
Here's the guy with the leaves, it's time to eat.*

Sloth can't you see I'm rushed off my feet?

Sloth crunched; munched; watched shadows play

Busy Agouti wasted away.

BARNYARD BIRDS

Barnyard birds choose not to be known as a flock
when they: gobble, quack, gabble and cluck
they are trying to make this clear.

Turkeys are titled a raft or a raffle
while chickens like to be addressed
as a brood, geese fly in a skein
yet when grounded are a nide or a gaggle.

Ducks are a plump when they fly
when they dive a dopping
a flush as they waddle
a baddling when they swim.

Disagreeable mallards have
names of their own
a sord on the water
and a sute on the land.

But the peafowls perch high
on this branch of creation
known as: a pride, a muster
or an ostentation.